EMMANUEL JOSEPH

The Innovator's Stage, How Public Speaking and Leadership Drive Action and Change

Copyright © 2025 by Emmanuel Joseph

All rights reserved. No part of this publication may be reproduced, stored or transmitted in any form or by any means, electronic, mechanical, photocopying, recording, scanning, or otherwise without written permission from the publisher. It is illegal to copy this book, post it to a website, or distribute it by any other means without permission.

First edition

This book was professionally typeset on Reedsy.
Find out more at reedsy.com

Contents

1	Chapter 1: The Power of Presence	1
2	Chapter 2: The Art of Storytelling	3
3	Chapter 3: Building Trust and Credibility	5
4	Chapter 4: The Science of Persuasion	7
5	Chapter 5: The Role of Non-Verbal Communication	9
6	Chapter 6: Crafting a Compelling Vision	11
7	Chapter 7: Inspiring Action through Vision	13
8	Chapter 8: Overcoming Resistance to Change	15
9	Chapter 9: Leading with Emotional Intelligence	17
10	Chapter 10: The Impact of Authentic Leadership	19
11	Chapter 11: Navigating Crisis and Conflict	21
12	Chapter 12: The Role of Ethics in Leadership	23
13	Chapter 13: The Importance of Adaptability	25
14	Chapter 14: Leading Diverse and Inclusive Teams	27
15	Chapter 15: Empowering Others	29
16	Chapter 16: The Power of Collaboration	31
17	Chapter 17: Sustaining Leadership Excellence	33

1

Chapter 1: The Power of Presence

In a world driven by ideas and communication, the ability to convey thoughts effectively has never been more critical. Public speaking is not just an art form; it's a tool for leadership and change. The power of presence, the ability to captivate and influence an audience, is the foundation upon which great leaders build their legacy. This chapter delves into the significance of presence and how it transforms mere words into a catalyst for action and change.

Presence is more than just standing on a stage and speaking; it's about commanding attention and engaging the audience on a deeper level. It involves the speaker's body language, tone of voice, and the ability to connect emotionally with the audience. A speaker with a powerful presence can make listeners feel seen, heard, and understood. This emotional connection is crucial for driving action, as people are more likely to be motivated and inspired by someone they feel a personal connection with.

Developing a strong presence requires self-awareness and practice. Leaders must understand their strengths and weaknesses and continuously work on improving their communication skills. This involves not only honing their public speaking abilities but also being mindful of their non-verbal cues and how they present themselves. By focusing on these aspects, leaders can create an authentic and compelling presence that resonates with their audience and drives them to take action.

The power of presence extends beyond the stage and into everyday interactions. Leaders who can effectively communicate their vision and inspire others are more likely to drive change and achieve their goals. This chapter explores various techniques and strategies for developing a powerful presence, from mastering the art of storytelling to using body language effectively. By understanding and harnessing the power of presence, leaders can become more effective communicators and change-makers, leaving a lasting impact on their audience and the world.

2

Chapter 2: The Art of Storytelling

S tories have the power to captivate, inspire, and drive change. They are the backbone of human communication, weaving together facts and emotions to create a compelling narrative. In this chapter, we explore how the art of storytelling can be harnessed by leaders to communicate their vision, rally support, and drive action.

Storytelling is an ancient art that transcends cultures and generations. It's a way to convey complex ideas in a relatable and memorable manner. Great leaders understand the power of stories and use them to illustrate their points, make connections with their audience, and leave a lasting impact. By crafting a well-told story, leaders can make their message more engaging and persuasive.

To become an effective storyteller, leaders must learn to identify the key elements of a good story: a clear beginning, middle, and end; relatable characters; and a conflict or challenge that is resolved in a satisfying way. These elements help to create a narrative arc that keeps the audience engaged and invested in the outcome. By incorporating personal anecdotes, leaders can add authenticity and emotional depth to their stories, making them more impactful.

In addition to crafting compelling stories, leaders must also learn to deliver them effectively. This involves mastering the use of voice, tone, and pacing to create suspense, emphasize key points, and maintain the audience's interest.

Body language and facial expressions also play a crucial role in storytelling, as they help to convey emotions and create a connection with the audience. By honing these skills, leaders can become more persuasive and influential communicators.

3

Chapter 3: Building Trust and Credibility

Trust and credibility are the cornerstones of effective leadership. Without them, even the most compelling message will fall flat. This chapter delves into the importance of building trust and credibility with an audience, and how leaders can achieve this through authenticity, transparency, and consistency.

Authenticity is the key to building trust. Leaders who are genuine and true to themselves are more likely to be trusted by their audience. This means being honest about their intentions, admitting their mistakes, and showing vulnerability when appropriate. By being authentic, leaders can create a sense of relatability and foster a deeper connection with their audience.

Transparency is another crucial element in building trust. Leaders must be open and honest about their decisions, actions, and the reasoning behind them. This involves sharing information and being willing to answer questions and address concerns. By being transparent, leaders can demonstrate their integrity and build credibility with their audience.

Consistency is also essential for building trust and credibility. Leaders must be consistent in their words and actions, following through on their promises and maintaining their principles even in the face of challenges. This consistency helps to establish a track record of reliability, which in turn builds trust and credibility with the audience.

In this chapter, we explore various strategies for building trust and credibility, from demonstrating authenticity and transparency to maintaining consistency in words and actions. By focusing on these elements, leaders can create a strong foundation for their communication and drive meaningful change.

4

Chapter 4: The Science of Persuasion

Persuasion is both an art and a science, and understanding the principles behind it can greatly enhance a leader's ability to influence others. This chapter delves into the psychological aspects of persuasion, exploring techniques that can help leaders effectively sway their audience and drive action.

The science of persuasion is rooted in understanding human behavior and motivation. People are influenced by various factors, including social proof, authority, and reciprocity. By leveraging these principles, leaders can create compelling arguments that resonate with their audience. For example, demonstrating expertise and authority on a subject can establish credibility and make the audience more likely to accept the leader's message.

Social proof, or the idea that people tend to follow the actions of others, is another powerful persuasive tool. Leaders can use testimonials, endorsements, and success stories to show that others have already embraced their vision, making it more appealing to the audience. Similarly, the principle of reciprocity, which suggests that people are more likely to respond positively to someone who has done something for them, can be used to build goodwill and encourage cooperation.

This chapter also explores the role of emotion in persuasion. People are more likely to be influenced by messages that evoke strong emotions, whether it's excitement, empathy, or urgency. By tapping into the audience's emotions, leaders can create a more impactful and memorable message. Through a combination of logical arguments and emotional appeals, leaders can become more persuasive and drive meaningful change.

5

Chapter 5: The Role of Non-Verbal Communication

Communication is not just about words; it encompasses a wide range of non-verbal cues that can significantly impact the effectiveness of a message. This chapter explores the role of non-verbal communication in public speaking and leadership, highlighting techniques that can enhance a leader's presence and influence.

Non-verbal communication includes body language, facial expressions, gestures, and eye contact. These cues can reinforce or undermine the spoken message, making it crucial for leaders to be mindful of their non-verbal signals. For example, maintaining eye contact with the audience can create a sense of connection and trust, while open and confident body language can convey authority and credibility.

Facial expressions play a key role in conveying emotions and building rapport with the audience. A genuine smile can create a positive impression, while a furrowed brow can signal concern or empathy. Leaders must learn to use their facial expressions intentionally to enhance their message and connect with their audience on an emotional level.

Gestures are another important aspect of non-verbal communication. Effective use of hand gestures can emphasize key points, illustrate concepts, and add energy to a speech. However, excessive or distracting gestures can detract from the message, so it's essential for leaders to strike a balance and use gestures purposefully.

This chapter provides practical tips and exercises for improving non-verbal communication skills. By becoming more aware of their non-verbal cues and practicing intentional body language, leaders can enhance their presence and become more effective communicators.

6

Chapter 6: Crafting a Compelling Vision

A compelling vision is the cornerstone of effective leadership. It serves as a guiding star, inspiring and motivating people to work towards a common goal. This chapter explores how leaders can craft and communicate a compelling vision that resonates with their audience and drives action.

A compelling vision is clear, ambitious, and aligned with the values and aspirations of the audience. It paints a vivid picture of the future and provides a sense of purpose and direction. Leaders must articulate their vision in a way that is both inspiring and attainable, creating a sense of excitement and urgency.

To craft a compelling vision, leaders must first understand their audience's needs, desires, and challenges. This involves conducting thorough research, listening to feedback, and engaging in meaningful conversations. By understanding what matters most to their audience, leaders can tailor their vision to address those concerns and aspirations.

Once the vision is crafted, leaders must communicate it effectively. This involves using storytelling, persuasive language, and non-verbal cues to convey the vision in a compelling and memorable way. Leaders must also be consistent in their messaging, reinforcing the vision through their actions and decisions.

This chapter provides practical strategies for crafting and communicating a compelling vision. By focusing on clarity, alignment, and communication, leaders can inspire their audience and drive meaningful change.

7

Chapter 7: Inspiring Action through Vision

Great leaders don't just share their vision—they inspire action. This chapter explores how leaders can motivate their audience to take meaningful steps towards achieving the vision, turning ideas into reality.

Inspiring action requires more than just presenting a compelling vision. Leaders must create a sense of urgency and show the audience the tangible benefits of taking action. This involves highlighting the positive impact that achieving the vision will have on individuals, communities, and the world at large. By painting a vivid picture of the future, leaders can ignite a sense of excitement and motivation in their audience.

One effective way to inspire action is through storytelling. Sharing success stories and examples of how others have already taken steps towards the vision can create a sense of possibility and encourage others to follow suit. Additionally, leaders should provide clear and actionable steps that the audience can take to contribute to the vision. By breaking down the process into manageable tasks, leaders can make it easier for people to get involved and make a difference.

In this chapter, we also explore the importance of celebrating progress and recognizing the contributions of others. Acknowledging and rewarding efforts can reinforce positive behavior and encourage continued action. By creating a culture of celebration and recognition, leaders can sustain momentum and drive long-term change.

8

Chapter 8: Overcoming Resistance to Change

Resistance to change is a natural human response, and effective leaders must be equipped to address and overcome it. This chapter delves into the common sources of resistance and provides strategies for leading through change with empathy and resilience.

People resist change for various reasons, including fear of the unknown, loss of control, and attachment to the status quo. Leaders must first understand these underlying concerns and address them with empathy. This involves actively listening to the audience, acknowledging their fears, and providing reassurance. By showing that they understand and care about the audience's concerns, leaders can build trust and create a more supportive environment for change.

Effective communication is crucial in overcoming resistance. Leaders should be transparent about the reasons for change and the benefits it will bring. Providing clear and consistent information can help alleviate uncertainty and build confidence in the vision. Additionally, involving the audience in the change process and giving them a sense of ownership can reduce resistance and increase buy-in.

In this chapter, we also explore the importance of resilience in leadership. Change can be challenging, and leaders must be prepared to face setbacks and obstacles. By staying resilient and maintaining a positive outlook, leaders can inspire their audience to persevere and stay committed to the vision.

9

Chapter 9: Leading with Emotional Intelligence

Emotional intelligence (EI) is a critical component of effective leadership. This chapter explores the role of EI in public speaking and leadership, highlighting how leaders can use their emotional awareness to connect with their audience and drive change.

Emotional intelligence involves the ability to recognize, understand, and manage one's own emotions and the emotions of others. Leaders with high EI are better equipped to navigate complex social interactions and build strong relationships. They can empathize with their audience, respond to emotional cues, and create a positive and supportive atmosphere.

One key aspect of EI is self-awareness. Leaders must be in tune with their own emotions and understand how they impact their behavior and communication. This self-awareness allows leaders to manage their emotions effectively and remain composed under pressure. Additionally, self-regulation enables leaders to stay focused and maintain a positive attitude, even in challenging situations.

Empathy is another crucial component of EI. By understanding and sharing the feelings of others, leaders can build rapport and trust with their audience. This involves actively listening, showing genuine concern, and responding with compassion. Empathetic leaders can create a sense of connection and inspire loyalty and commitment.

This chapter provides practical tips for developing and applying emotional intelligence in leadership. By enhancing their EI, leaders can become more effective communicators, build stronger relationships, and drive meaningful change.

10

Chapter 10: The Impact of Authentic Leadership

Authentic leadership is about being true to oneself and leading with integrity. This chapter explores the impact of authentic leadership on driving action and change, highlighting the importance of aligning words and actions with core values.

Authentic leaders are genuine and transparent, and they lead with a sense of purpose and passion. They are true to their values and principles, and they inspire others by setting a positive example. This authenticity creates trust and credibility, making it easier for leaders to influence and motivate their audience.

One key aspect of authentic leadership is self-awareness. Authentic leaders have a deep understanding of their strengths, weaknesses, and values. This self-awareness allows them to lead with confidence and humility, acknowledging their limitations and seeking input from others. By being open and honest, authentic leaders create an environment of trust and collaboration.

Another important aspect of authentic leadership is consistency. Authentic leaders align their words and actions with their values, and they consistently demonstrate their commitment to the vision. This consistency reinforces their credibility and builds trust with their audience.

In this chapter, we also explore the importance of vulnerability in authentic leadership. Authentic leaders are not afraid to show vulnerability and admit their mistakes. This vulnerability creates a sense of relatability and fosters deeper connections with the audience. By being authentic and vulnerable, leaders can inspire others to be their true selves and contribute to the vision.

11

Chapter 11: Navigating Crisis and Conflict

Leadership is tested in times of crisis and conflict. This chapter explores how leaders can navigate challenging situations with grace, resilience, and effectiveness, turning adversity into an opportunity for growth and change.

In times of crisis, clear and decisive communication is crucial. Leaders must provide accurate and timely information, addressing concerns and calming fears. This involves being transparent about the situation, acknowledging uncertainties, and outlining the steps being taken to address the crisis. By maintaining open lines of communication, leaders can build trust and foster a sense of stability.

Conflict is an inevitable part of leadership, and effective leaders must be skilled in managing and resolving disputes. This involves understanding the root causes of conflict, actively listening to all parties involved, and finding common ground. Leaders should approach conflict with empathy and a focus on collaboration, seeking solutions that address the needs and concerns of everyone involved. By resolving conflicts constructively, leaders can strengthen relationships and create a more cohesive and productive team.

This chapter also explores the importance of resilience in crisis and conflict management. Leaders must remain calm and composed, even in the face of adversity. This involves staying focused on the bigger picture, maintaining a positive attitude, and being adaptable in the face of changing circumstances. By demonstrating resilience, leaders can inspire confidence and motivate others to persevere.

12

Chapter 12: The Role of Ethics in Leadership

Ethics are the foundation of effective and responsible leadership. This chapter delves into the importance of ethical leadership and how leaders can uphold integrity and accountability in their actions and decisions.

Ethical leadership involves making decisions that are fair, transparent, and aligned with core values. Leaders must prioritize the well-being of their team, organization, and society as a whole. This involves considering the long-term impact of their actions and being accountable for the outcomes. By adhering to ethical principles, leaders can build trust and credibility, both within their organization and with external stakeholders.

One key aspect of ethical leadership is leading by example. Leaders must model the behavior they expect from others, demonstrating integrity and accountability in their actions. This involves being honest, keeping promises, and taking responsibility for mistakes. By setting a positive example, leaders can create a culture of ethics and integrity within their organization.

Another important aspect of ethical leadership is fostering an environment where ethical behavior is encouraged and rewarded. This involves creating clear ethical guidelines, providing training and resources, and promoting a culture of transparency and open communication. Leaders should also be proactive in addressing unethical behavior and ensuring that consequences are fair and consistent.

This chapter provides practical strategies for practicing ethical leadership, from making values-based decisions to creating an ethical organizational culture. By prioritizing ethics, leaders can build a strong foundation for sustainable success and positive impact.

13

Chapter 13: The Importance of Adaptability

In a rapidly changing world, adaptability is a critical leadership skill. This chapter explores the importance of being flexible and open to change, and how leaders can develop and apply adaptability to drive innovation and success.

Adaptable leaders are able to navigate uncertainty and embrace new challenges with a positive and proactive mindset. They are open to learning and growth, willing to adjust their strategies and approaches in response to changing circumstances. This flexibility allows them to stay ahead of the curve and seize new opportunities.

One key aspect of adaptability is the ability to manage change effectively. Leaders must be skilled in leading their team through transitions, providing clear direction and support. This involves communicating the reasons for change, addressing concerns, and involving the team in the process. By fostering a culture of adaptability, leaders can create an environment where innovation and continuous improvement thrive.

Another important aspect of adaptability is resilience. Adaptable leaders are able to bounce back from setbacks and view challenges as opportunities for growth. They maintain a positive attitude and stay focused on their goals, even in the face of adversity. By demonstrating resilience, leaders can inspire their team to persevere and stay committed to the vision.

This chapter provides practical tips for developing adaptability, from staying curious and open-minded to embracing change and uncertainty. By cultivating adaptability, leaders can drive innovation, stay relevant, and achieve long-term success.

14

Chapter 14: Leading Diverse and Inclusive Teams

Diversity and inclusion are essential for fostering innovation and driving success. This chapter explores how leaders can create and lead diverse and inclusive teams, leveraging the strengths and perspectives of all team members.

Diverse teams bring together individuals with different backgrounds, experiences, and perspectives. This diversity of thought can lead to more creative solutions and better decision-making. However, creating a truly inclusive environment requires more than just assembling a diverse team. Leaders must actively work to ensure that all team members feel valued, respected, and included.

Inclusive leadership involves creating a culture where everyone feels comfortable sharing their ideas and perspectives. This involves actively listening to all voices, addressing biases, and promoting a sense of belonging. Leaders should also provide opportunities for professional development and growth, ensuring that all team members have the resources and support they need to succeed.

Another important aspect of leading diverse and inclusive teams is fostering open and respectful communication. Leaders should encourage open dialogue and create spaces where team members can discuss and address any concerns or challenges. By promoting a culture of transparency and inclusion, leaders can build stronger and more cohesive teams.

This chapter provides practical strategies for creating and leading diverse and inclusive teams, from addressing unconscious biases to promoting inclusive practices and policies. By prioritizing diversity and inclusion, leaders can drive innovation, enhance team performance, and achieve greater success.

15

Chapter 15: Empowering Others

Empowerment is a fundamental aspect of effective leadership. This chapter explores how leaders can empower their team members, fostering a sense of ownership, confidence, and motivation that drives action and change.

Empowering others involves providing them with the autonomy and resources they need to succeed. This means trusting team members to take ownership of their tasks and decisions, while offering support and guidance as needed. Leaders should encourage a culture of accountability, where team members feel responsible for their contributions and take pride in their work.

One key aspect of empowerment is recognizing and leveraging individual strengths. Leaders should take the time to understand the unique skills and talents of each team member and provide opportunities for them to shine. By aligning tasks and responsibilities with individual strengths, leaders can enhance team performance and job satisfaction.

Another important aspect of empowerment is providing opportunities for growth and development. Leaders should offer training, mentorship, and career advancement opportunities to help team members reach their full potential. By investing in their team's development, leaders can create a more skilled and motivated workforce.

This chapter provides practical strategies for empowering others, from delegating tasks effectively to providing constructive feedback and recognition.

By fostering a culture of empowerment, leaders can inspire their team to take initiative, innovate, and drive meaningful change.

16

Chapter 16: The Power of Collaboration

Collaboration is essential for achieving collective goals and driving innovation. This chapter explores how leaders can foster a collaborative environment, bringing together diverse perspectives and skills to achieve greater success.

Effective collaboration involves creating a culture of open communication, trust, and mutual respect. Leaders should encourage team members to share their ideas and perspectives, and actively listen to each other's input. This involves creating spaces for open dialogue, whether through regular team meetings, brainstorming sessions, or digital collaboration tools.

Leaders should also promote a sense of shared purpose and common goals. By aligning the team's efforts towards a clear and compelling vision, leaders can create a sense of unity and motivation. This involves setting clear expectations, providing regular updates on progress, and celebrating collective achievements.

Another important aspect of collaboration is leveraging the strengths of each team member. Leaders should recognize and appreciate the unique skills and contributions of each individual, and create opportunities for them to work together in complementary ways. By fostering a culture of collaboration, leaders can tap into the collective intelligence and creativity of the team, driving innovation and achieving greater success.

This chapter provides practical tips for fostering collaboration, from building trust and communication to creating a shared vision and leveraging team strengths. By prioritizing collaboration, leaders can create a more cohesive and effective team, and drive meaningful change.

17

Chapter 17: Sustaining Leadership Excellence

Sustaining leadership excellence requires continuous learning, growth, and adaptation. This final chapter explores how leaders can maintain and enhance their leadership skills, staying effective and relevant in a rapidly changing world.

One key aspect of sustaining leadership excellence is a commitment to lifelong learning. Leaders should continually seek out new knowledge, skills, and perspectives, whether through formal education, professional development, or personal exploration. This involves staying informed about industry trends, seeking feedback from others, and embracing a growth mindset.

Another important aspect is self-care and well-being. Leadership can be demanding, and leaders must prioritize their physical, mental, and emotional health. This involves setting boundaries, managing stress, and maintaining a healthy work-life balance. By taking care of themselves, leaders can sustain their energy and resilience, and continue to lead effectively.

Leaders should also cultivate a network of mentors, peers, and supporters. Building strong relationships with other leaders and professionals can provide valuable insights, support, and opportunities for growth. This involves actively seeking out and nurturing these connections, and being open to learning from others.

Finally, sustaining leadership excellence involves reflecting on and refining one's leadership approach. Leaders should regularly assess their performance, seek feedback, and identify areas for improvement. By being proactive in their development, leaders can stay adaptable and effective, and continue to drive meaningful change.

This chapter provides practical strategies for sustaining leadership excellence, from continuous learning and self-care to building a support network and reflective practice. By committing to their ongoing development, leaders can maintain their impact and effectiveness, and continue to inspire and drive action and change.

The Innovator's Stage: How Public Speaking and Leadership Drive Action and Change

In today's rapidly evolving world, the ability to communicate effectively and lead with conviction is more important than ever. "The Innovator's Stage" delves into the powerful intersection of public speaking and leadership, revealing how these two skills can drive meaningful action and create lasting change.

Across 17 engaging chapters, this book explores the art and science of effective communication, from mastering the power of presence and storytelling to building trust and credibility. It provides practical insights into the psychological principles of persuasion, the role of non-verbal communication, and the importance of emotional intelligence.

Readers will discover strategies for crafting and communicating a compelling vision, inspiring action, and overcoming resistance to change. The book also highlights the significance of ethical leadership, adaptability, and leading diverse and inclusive teams. By empowering others and fostering collaboration, leaders can unlock the full potential of their teams and drive innovation.

"The Innovator's Stage" is a comprehensive guide for anyone looking to enhance their public speaking and leadership skills. Whether you're a seasoned leader or an aspiring change-maker, this book offers valuable tools and strategies to help you make a positive impact on your audience and the world.

www.ingramcontent.com/pod-product-compliance
Lightning Source LLC
LaVergne TN
LVHW010441070526
838199LV00066B/6133